Edition Schott

Alvin Singleton

b.1940

Ishirini

for Two Violins

ED 30072

www.schott-music.com

Mainz · London · Madrid · New York · Paris · Prague · Tokyo · Toronto

World Premiere
September 1, 2003
Music from Angel Fire Chamber Music Festival, New Mexico
Ida Kavafian & Daniel Phillips, violins

Commissioned by and dedicated to Music from Angel Fire's 20th Anniversary Season,
with the support of The Bruce E. Howden, Jr. American Composers Project.

ISHIRINI
for two violins

Alvin Singleton (2003)

Edition Schott

Alvin Singleton

b.1940

Ishirini

for Two Violins

ED 30072

www.schott-music.com

Mainz · London · Madrid · New York · Paris · Prague · Tokyo · Toronto

World Premiere
September 1, 2003
Music from Angel Fire Chamber Music Festival, New Mexico
Ida Kavafian & Daniel Phillips, violins

Commissioned by and dedicated to Music from Angel Fire's 20th Anniversary Season, with the support of The Bruce E. Howden, Jr. American Composers Project.

ISHIRINI
for two violins

Alvin Singleton (2003)

ED 30072

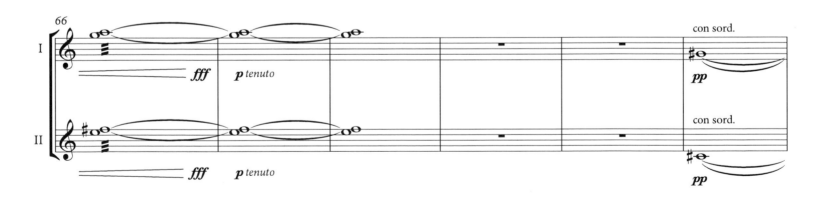

MacDowell Colony, NH
August 28, 2003

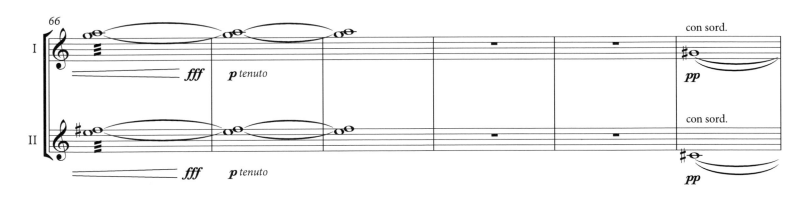

MacDowell Colony, NH
August 28, 2003